THE GREAT WHALES COLORING ALBUM

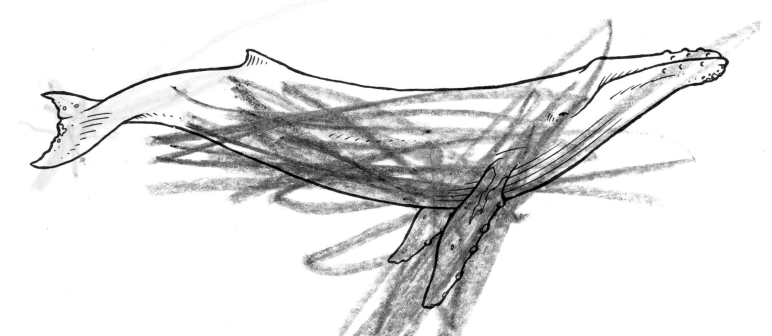

Designed & Illustrated by Daniel Smith

Written by Malcolm Whyte

TROUBADOR PRESS
a subsidiary of
PRICE STERN SLOAN
Los Angeles

Text copyright © 1987 by Word Play, Inc.
Illustrations copyright © 1987 by Daniel Smith
Published by TROUBADOR PRESS, a subsidiary of Price Stern Sloan, Inc.
360 North La Cienega Boulevard, Los Angeles, California 90048

10 9 8 7 6 5   ISBN: 0-8431-1953-5

HUMPBACK WHALE

Megaptera novaeanglie

Length: 50-60 feet (15-19 m)   Weight: 45-53 tons (45,700-53,800 kg)

Range: all oceans of the world

As the sun moves south in the winter skies, humpback whales all over the world stream toward warmer waters. The Pacific humpback, for instance, cruises from Alaska, where it feeds all summer, to Hawaii in the winter. There the whales mate, give birth to their young and play from December to April, much to the delight of whale watchers. Gliding between the green, palm-lined islands, they will suddenly breach (jump into the air), flashing their white flippers against their powerful, shiny black skin.

Humpbacks get their name from the way they curve their backs above the waterline before they sound (dive). They are easily recognized by the hairy bumps on their heads, notched flukes (tail fins) and long, knobby flippers that run almost one-third the length of their bodies.

Humpbacks are also well known for their unique underwater singing. The song is made by the male, and lasts up to twenty minutes. It has a wide variety and range of tones. Hearing recordings of their moving, soulful melodies both increases our knowledge of these gentle giants of the deep and deepens the mystery that surrounds them.

SEI WHALE

Balaenoptera borealis

Length: 60-65 feet (18-20 m)   Weight: 24-26 tons (24,400-26,400 kg)

Range: all oceans of the world; avoids ice packs

Every day, for all of its nearly seventy years of life, the sei hunts for food. Sliding through choppy waters, mouth open, it takes great quantities of water and fish into its expanded throat, where the material passes through massive walls of baleen. Baleen are thin, fibrous plates that hang from the whale's upper jaw instead of teeth. These long triangle shapes have smooth outer edges and frayed, hairlike inner edges. Each plate meshes with its neighbor to form a natural strainer. Small crustaceans, anchovies, capelin, pollack, herring, cod or sardines in the sei's diet slip easily into the whale's mouth, only to get stuck against the screen of baleen as the water is forced back out. The sei scours the fish from its baleen and is ready to feed again.

In the middle of its hunt, drumming motors from a boat warn the sei of the craft's approach. Being the fastest swimmer of all whales, it can outrun many boats with speeds of up to 24 mph (38 kph). But this time, instead of fleeing, the sei sounds for ten minutes while the ship steams by. Then the sea is quiet again, except for the rippling rush of the mighty sei's renewed hunt for food.

FIN WHALE

Balaenoptera physalus

Length: 70-80 feet (21-24 m)   Weight: 40-50 tons (40,600-50,800 kg)

Range: all oceans of the world; avoids shallow coastal waters

An upright dorsal fin swiftly cuts the water, then slows. Long, sleek and graceful, the pregnant female fin whale — known also as a "finback" — knows that her time is near. For eleven and one-half months the mother fin has carried her unborn baby. Now, with its birth, things happen fast.

First, the young whale's umbilical cord is severed. It will wither away, leaving the baby with a belly button, just like humans have. Then the mother pushes her calf to the surface for its first breath of fresh sea air. This is no small baby, weighing nearly 4 tons (4064 kg) and running 21 feet (6.5 m) long! Like all mammals, the calf will feed on its mother's rich milk. A year will pass before it can catch its own food, while it stays with, plays with and learns from its mother.

Where once there were over 900,000 fin whales in the world, today they number about 150,000. With human protection, however, the baby fin will grow to be a parent, too, and help to increase the population in its 75- to 100-year life.

BOTTLENOSE DOLPHIN

Tursiops truncatus

Length: 10 feet (3 m)   Weight: 450 lbs. (204 kg)

Range: all temperate and tropical seas

Most marine animals live with a scarcity of light. Near the surface of the water visibility is limited to a few paces in all but the very clearest water. Below 500 feet (150 m), all light fades to inky darkness, making sight impossible. Hearing, on the other hand, is actually improved underwater because sound travels faster, farther and more efficiently. Cetaceans have taken advantage of these facts by developing echolocation to get around in their world.

Echolocation is the sonar of the whales. By sending out sounds and interpreting the returning echoes, they can tell where they are, where and what prey is near, and are able to talk with each other.

Dolphins have especially well-developed communication capabilities. Their three dozen species make them the largest family of cetaceans. The most familiar is the bottlenose dolphin, which we often see leaping and dashing through the tanks at marine parks, or smiling and chattering like Flipper on television. These highly intelligent, playful sea mammals adapt readily to captivity. The fact that they welcome human company gives us all an important chance to know, love and respect the whale family first-hand.

GRAY WHALE

Eschrichtius robustus

Length: 45 feet (13 m)　　　　　　　Weight: 35 tons (35,600 kg)

Range: Bering and Chukchi Seas

Great whales are noted for great migrations — and the gray whale has the longest trek of any mammal. To journey from their feeding grounds near the Arctic to the protected lagoons of Baja California, they travel 7000 miles (11,000 km)! After feasting all summer on crustaceans and small school fish, the whales have built up heavy layers of insulating, and nourishing, blubber (fat). Now they are ready for the six-month Alaska-to-Mexico journey.

Led by pregnant females, the grays need to reach the warmer waters to ensure the survival of their nearly blubberless babies. They will eat little at this time except for some microorganisms scraped from kelp (seaweed) fronds. After calving, slimmer than before, they head north again toward their feeding grounds to rebuild their protective blubber.

Whale watchers along the Pacific coast of the United States can count on seeing grays roaming south from November through February, then back again from March through May. They will see more whales, too, as the eastern North Pacific population of grays has grown from only a few thousand fifty years ago to over 17,000 today. And if the observers are lucky, they may see a gray "spyhopping," when it "stands" in the water to look around. It's one way for a whale to watch the whale watchers!

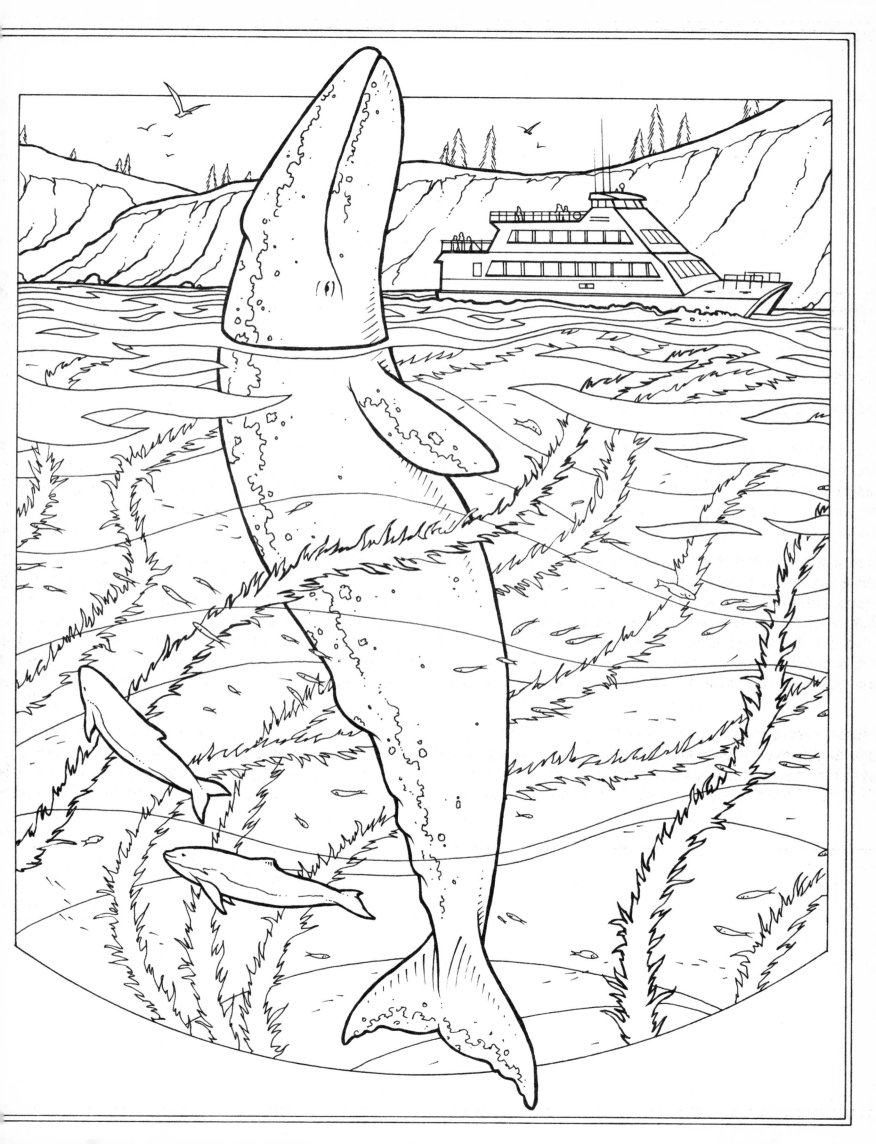

BOWHEAD WHALE

Balaena mysticetus

Length: 65 feet (20 m)   Weight: 65 tons (66,000 kg)

Range: Arctic waters of the Northern Hemisphere

Seventy-one percent of the world's surface is covered by seas, and the bowhead whale inhabits the coldest one. A rich source of oil — nearly one hundred barrels from a large bowhead — these stocky baleens were hunted to near extinction by whalers, yet they continue to live.

Bowheads live in the icy waters of the Arctic, where they feed on crustaceans. Unlike their rorqual whale cousins, they have no pleated, expandable throat with which to gulp food. Instead, they drift slowly through the water, with their huge lips curled up to strain in their prey. Now and then they close the lips over their fourteen-foot-long (4.3 m) baleen plates, force the water back out and clean the food off of the fine strands. Like all mammals, bowheads cannot drink seawater. The water they need comes from processing, or "burning," the fat in their diet.

Swimming and diving in their harsh Arctic environment can sometimes be a threat; bowheads may come up for air and find the surface covered with ice. But with their broad, strong backs, these whales can break through ice caps of up to twelve inches (30.5 m) thick to make a breathing hole. For this reason, bowheads are sometimes found accompanied by the smaller beluga, helping it survive.

MINKE WHALE

Balaenoptera acutostrata

Length: 30 feet (9 m)   Weight: 8 tons (8100 kg)

Range: all oceans, with concentration in temperate waters

A small fishing party is pleasantly surprised by the breaching of a nearby young minke whale. As it arcs back into the waves, it displays the pure white band on its flippers which is unique to this whale. Although this boat is no threat, others are. The minke is the most commercially hunted whale; thousands are still killed yearly.

Also called the "little piked whale" and "lesser rorqual," it is the smallest of the rorqual group that includes the blue, fin, sei, Bryde's, gray and humpback whales. This group is distinguishable by the numerous throat grooves that expand to allow the mammal to take in large quantities of food. Rorquals are considered to be the most modern, or recently evolved, of all the whales.

Scientists believe that over sixty million years ago a land animal re-entered the ocean; perhaps for protection and less competition for food. It took about twenty million more years for the mammal to evolve into a new order, Cetacea, which includes whales, dolphins and porpoises. Fossils of the ancestors of our present-day whales have been found to be forty million years old.

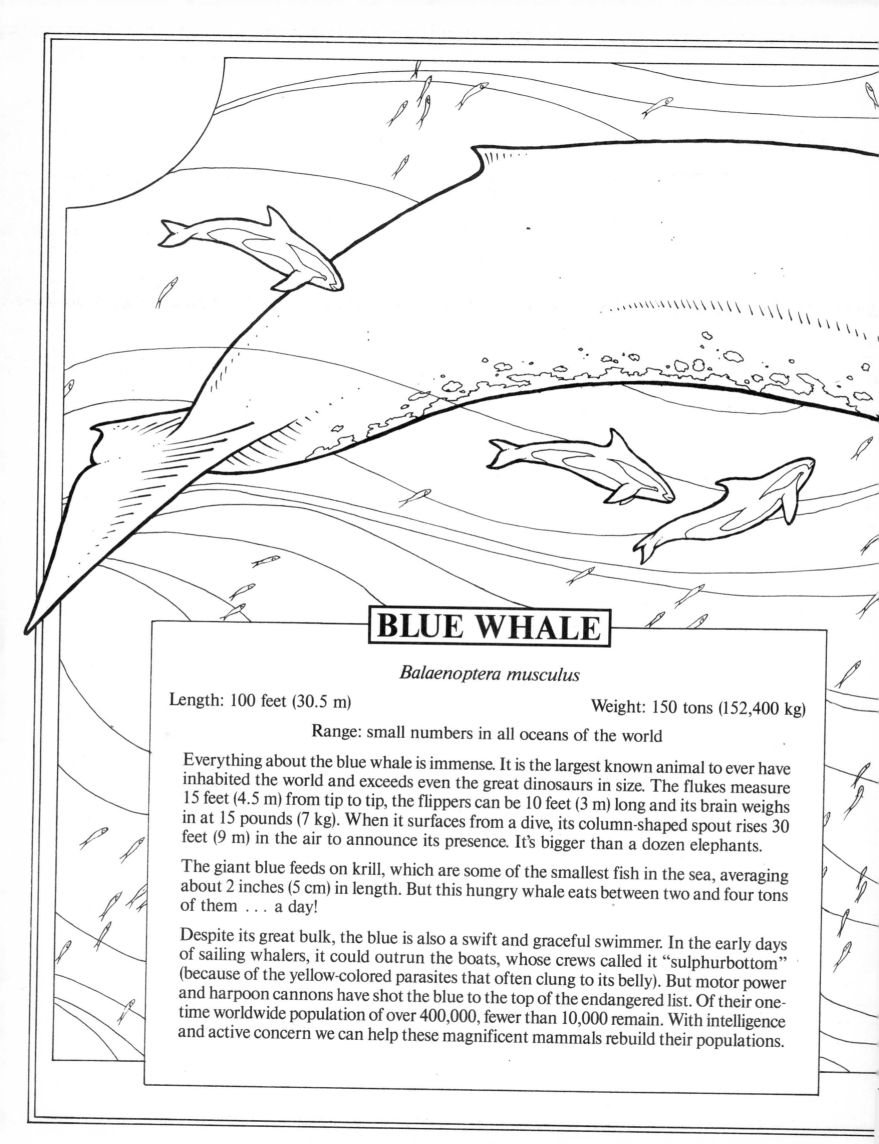

BLUE WHALE

Balaenoptera musculus

Length: 100 feet (30.5 m)   Weight: 150 tons (152,400 kg)

Range: small numbers in all oceans of the world

Everything about the blue whale is immense. It is the largest known animal to ever have inhabited the world and exceeds even the great dinosaurs in size. The flukes measure 15 feet (4.5 m) from tip to tip, the flippers can be 10 feet (3 m) long and its brain weighs in at 15 pounds (7 kg). When it surfaces from a dive, its column-shaped spout rises 30 feet (9 m) in the air to announce its presence. It's bigger than a dozen elephants.

The giant blue feeds on krill, which are some of the smallest fish in the sea, averaging about 2 inches (5 cm) in length. But this hungry whale eats between two and four tons of them . . . a day!

Despite its great bulk, the blue is also a swift and graceful swimmer. In the early days of sailing whalers, it could outrun the boats, whose crews called it "sulphurbottom" (because of the yellow-colored parasites that often clung to its belly). But motor power and harpoon cannons have shot the blue to the top of the endangered list. Of their one-time worldwide population of over 400,000, fewer than 10,000 remain. With intelligence and active concern we can help these magnificent mammals rebuild their populations.

BAIRD'S BEAKED WHALE

Berardius bairdii

Length: 40 feet (12 m)   Weight: 12 tons (12,200 kg)

Range: North Pacific, from Japan to Southern California

A small band of Baird's beaked whales races through the blue-green Pacific sea hunting for fish and squid. The water slips easily over their efficient, sleek-skinned shapes as they snap their prey into toothed, undershot jaws. Most whales herd together, feeding, migrating, reproducing, always communicating with each other. Baird's are deep divers who swim in groups from six to forty in number. Also called the "northern giant bottlenosed whale," they migrate north in the summer and south in the winter following the movement of their food supply.

Baird's whale is one of several types of beaked and bottlenosed whale. It is named after Spencer F. Baird, Secretary of the Smithsonian Institution from 1878 to 1887. Many species are rare, such as Hector's, Longman's, Arnoux's, Shepard's and Cuvier's beaked whales, and not much is known about them. Because they are scarce and live in remote areas, they are studied only from photographs, skeleton remains or stranded specimens. They are not captured for live study.

NARWHAL

Monodon monoceros

Length: 13-15 feet (4-4.5 m)   Weight: 2000-3500 lbs. (907-1590 kg)

Range: Arctic and polar seas

If you were a medieval sailor and came upon the remains of a narwhal, you might think that you had discovered a unicorn — and you might bring the spiraling ivory tusk back home as proof of your adventure. Historians believe that this is how the myth of the unicorn began.

The narwhal's tusk is actually a single tooth that grows from the skull out through its upper lip. Usually found only in the adult male, the curious spike reaches lengths of 8 feet (2.5 m), and always twists counter-clockwise. Its purpose is a mystery, however, because it is too awkward for battle and too impractical for food gathering.

Besides the bowhead whale, the narwhal is the only other cetacean to spend its lifetime in Arctic waters. It has no reason to leave, as its deep-water icy environment offers a rich diet of squid, halibut, cod, flounder, rockfish, shrimp and crab.

RIGHT WHALE

Balaena glacialis

Length: 50-60 feet (15-18 m)   Weight: 70-100 tons (71,100-101,600 kg)

Range: all temperate waters

"Thar she blows!" came the cry from the old sailing ship's lookout as he spied the spout of a right whale. For centuries, whales have been hunted for oil, whalebone and food for people and pets. Right whales are so named because they were the right ones to catch: they are slow, very rich in oily blubber and float when killed, making them easier to handle. Even though whaling has been greatly reduced — or completely stopped — by most nations, the right whale is one of the most endangered species of whales.

The whale's spout results from a sudden exhaling after the whale surfaces. Warm moist air from its lungs and some sea water gathered around its blowhole mix with the cooler sea air to create a column of steam that can be seen for miles around.

With homely-looking (but natural) lumpy callosites on its head and a mean scowl caused by its large, down-curling lips, it is surprising to know that this baleen whale has a sense of humor. One of its most ingenious tricks is to raise its flukes as a sail, so it can be pushed by the breeze. Downwind it glides, only to swim back to where it started to catch another ride.

SPERM WHALE

Physeter macrocephalus

Length: 40-60 feet (13-18 m)   Weight: 18-50 tons (18,300-50,800 kg)

Range: all subtropic and temperate waters

Two of the most famous fictional sperm whales are Moby Dick, from Herman Melville's classic novel, and Monstro in Walt Disney's version of *Pinocchio*. Both have fierce reputations. With an enormous, square head, beady eyes and a rack of gigantic teeth, the sperm whale makes a frightening impression. Its battle, however, is not with man, but with the giant squid, its primary food source.

To pursue a meal, this largest of toothed whales may plunge to depths of almost a mile (1.5 km) and endure incredible pressure — up to 2600 pounds per square inch. Yet it swims back to the top, showing no ill effects (except for a few scars from the fight).

Inside the sperm whale's high forehead is the spermaceti organ, a mass of muscle and oil-filled tissue that changes density as the animal easily moves up and down the great depths. Studying this amazing capability helps scientists solve the problems that humans have in underwater deep diving.

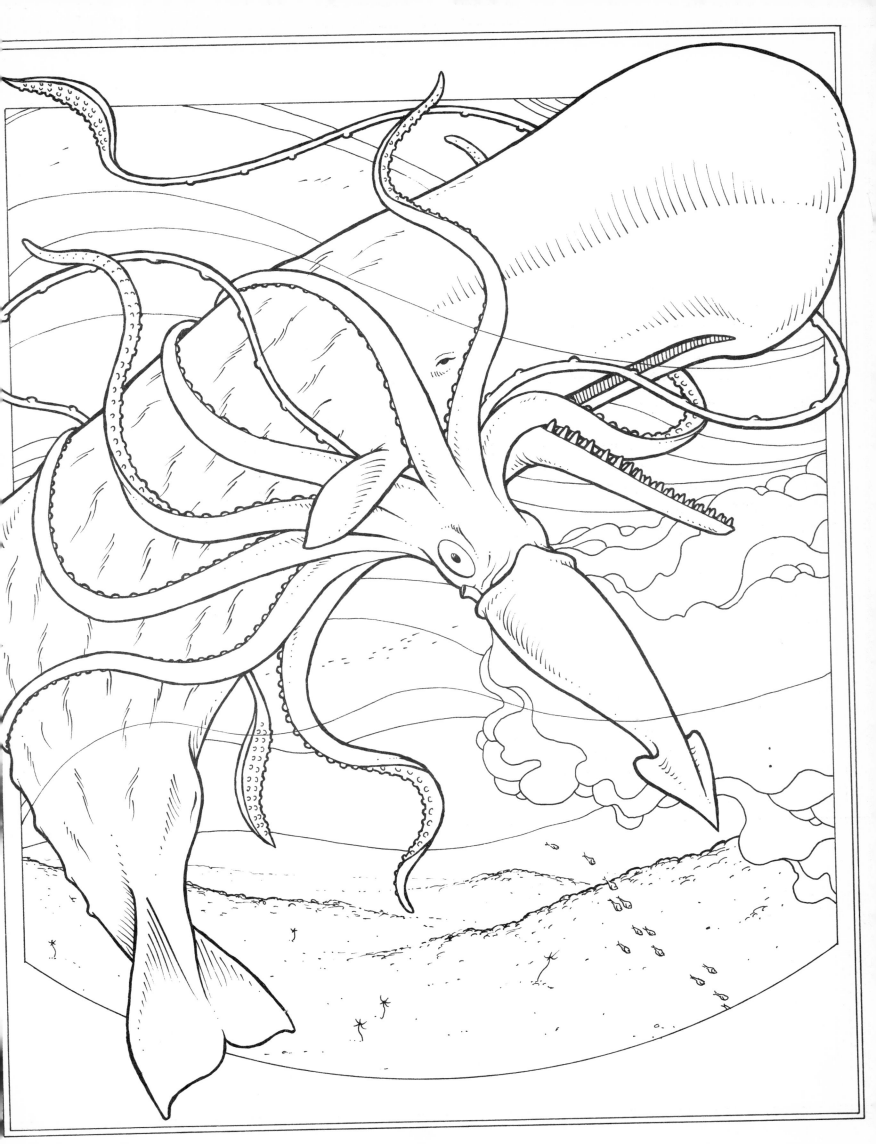

KILLER WHALE

Orcinus orcas

Length: 27-31 feet (8-9.5 m)   Weight: 5-9 tons (5100-9100 kg)

Range: all oceans

Tan, green and pearly gray reflections of the sloping hills rock back and forth along the stony shoreline. Suddenly, a killer whale bursts into the air, startling the basking sea lions. Safely ashore, they need not fear this spectacular black and white creature, but in the water it would be different.

The killer whale is the largest member of the dolphin family. Like its cousins it is an active, inquisitive mammal whose curiosity causes it to even approach small boats at close range. Although there is no record of human fatality due to an attacking killer whale, they are deadly predators of other large mammals. Swimming in packs, they hunt for porpoises, penguins, seals and sea lions, as well as fish and squid. Even the giant blue whale is not safe from their slashing, cone-shaped teeth.

"Orcas," as they are also called, keep in contact with each other by underwater vocalizations. Breaching is another way for them to know where they are by sighting landmarks. For whales in general, breaching can also aid in feeding, helping to wash down food and remove parasites, and it appears to be just plain fun — even for the killer whale.

BELUGA

Delphinapterus leucas

Length: 16 feet (5 m) Weight: 2400 lbs. (1000 kg)

Range: Arctic Ocean and nearby seas

A familiar chirping sound at the edge of the ice alerts a hungry polar bear. Several beluga whales have gathered to feed and talk, seemingly unaware that they might become a meal themselves. The three enemies of the beluga are: man, the killer whale and the polar bear. The bear waits near a clearing in the ice that has grown over the water. If the whale surfaces in the hole to breathe, the polar bear will stun it with its mighty paw and drag the meal onto the ice.

Belugas are very social animals who herd together, sometimes by the thousands. Their thick layers of blubber insulate them in their frigid habitat, but they migrate to warmer waters to breed. Born brown in color with gray spots, belugas turn snowy white as adults, and they are sometimes called "the white whale." Because their loud chattering could even be heard through the hulls of the old whaling ships, the crews also named these toothed whales "sea canaries."

The darkening evening sky brings out the aurora borealis, or northern lights. Seeing that this group of belugas is staying well out of reach, the bear turns and pads away. The sea canaries continue their serenade uninterrupted while the lights flash orange, blue, yellow and green over the frozen land.

HUMPHREY

One early October day in 1985, a young humpback strayed from his migrating pod. Instead of going south, he turned east into San Francisco Bay. He continued east through San Pablo Bay up Cache Slough, off the Sacramento River, where he stopped. The thousands who first cheered at this rare sight now worried about "Humphrey," as they called the whale. Would the fresh water hurt his eyes and skin? Would he starve? Would he get stuck? Something had to be done. Fast!

A rescue team was organized. People banging pipes in the water brought their boats in behind Humphrey. Another boat playing sounds of feeding humpbacks into the water ran in front. Bit by bit he moved toward the ocean. Just as he got to the Golden Gate Bridge, he turned inland again, but the little fleet blocked his way. With a flip of his tail, he dove under the bridge, south toward the migrating herd.

Humphrey's nearly four-week visit made history. Scientists studied him. The media recorded him. And Humphrey won the hearts of millions who, by word and action, helped save the whale.

HUMPHREY'S INLAND JOURNEY

WHALE'S ANATOMY
(Bryde's Whale)

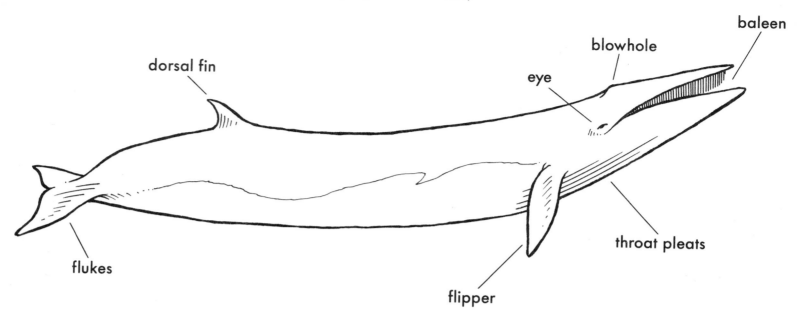

GLOSSARY

baleen: fibrous plates attached to the upper jaw of certain whales for filtering food organisms from sea water.

blowhole: a nostril at the highest point on the head of a whale.

cetacean: of or belonging to the order Cetacea, which includes marine mammals such as whales and dolphins.

cetologist: one who studies the zoology of cetaceans.

crustaceans: water animals of the class Crustacea, including shrimp, crabs, lobster and barnacles.

evolve: to develop or change gradually.

flukes: the two parts of the horizontal tail of a cetacean.

krill: small marine crustaceans, constituting the principal food of baleen whales.

microorganisms: animals or plants of microscopic size.

migration: the act of moving seasonally from one region to another.

parasite: an organism that lives on another organism while giving nothing to the host's survival.

pod: family units of whales or dolphins.

rorqual: any of baleen whales having long grooves on the throat and a small, pointed dorsal fin.

sounding: to dive swiftly.

For additional whale information, write to:

WHALE CENTER
3929 Piedmont Ave.
Oakland, CA 94611

GREENPEACE U.S.A.
1611 Connecticut Ave. N.W.
Washington, DC 20009

THE COUSTEAU SOCIETY
930 W. 21st St.
Norfolk, VA 23517